Read All About

THE

OCEANS

by Jaclyn Jaycox

Raintree is an imprint of Capstone Global Library Limited, a company incorporated in England and Wales having its registered office at 264 Banbury Road, Oxford, OX2 7DY – Registered company number: 6695582

www.raintree.co.uk
myorders@raintree.co.uk

Designed by Kayla Rossow
Original illustrations © Capstone Global Library Limited 2021
Picture research by Morgan Walters
Production by Katy LaVigne
Originated by Capstone Global Library Ltd
Printed and bound in India

978 1 3982 0324 2 (hardback)
978 1 3982 0323 5 (paperback)

British Library Cataloguing in Publication Data
A full catalogue record for this book is available from the British Library.

Acknowledgements
We would like to thank the following for permission to reproduce photographs: iStockphoto: FangXiaNuo, top 31, SolStock, bottom 30; Newscom: Flip Nicklin / Minden Pictures, top right 18; Shutterstock: Aila Images, bottom 31, Alessandro De Maddalena, top right 15, Alex Stemmer, middle right 23, Alizada Studios, bottom 27, Anastasiya Bleskina, (watercolour) Cover, Animas Photography, 7, best works, bottom 9, Brett Allen, bottom Cover, CChamorro, middle 10, Christopher Wood, bottom 19, Damsea, bottom left 23, Daoqian Lin, top left 30, DidGason, 24, Dmitry Tkachenko Photo, bottom 5, Ethan Daniels, bottom 10, FloridaStock, bottom 17, Gael GAUTH, top 14, Greg Amptman, top left 15, Incredible Arctic, top 17, Irina Markova, middle, Jemastock, design element, JohnL, top 19, Jukkis, top 6, Julia Kuleshova, top 25, Kelvin Degree, design element, Leonardo Gonzalez, bottom 15, Lukasz Szwaj, top 13, Lycia W, top right 29, Marisa Estivill, bottom 13, Maxim Safronov, middle 21, Naoto Shinkai, bottom 11, Pearl-diver, top 21, photoneye, 28, polarman, bottom 26, Pyty, 16, ReVelStockArt, design elements, Rich Carey, bottom 6, top left 23, robert_s, top 5, robuart, 4, RWBrooks, middle 9, S.Borisov, top 9, Samjaw, middle left 29, Sean Pavone, top 22, Seb c'est bien, bottom 22, Sergey 402, top 27, Smit, top right Cover, Steve Allen, top 26, Tainar, 1, Tarpan, bottom 25, TeaGraphicDesign, 12, 20, Thomas Kammer, bottom 14, tunasalmon, top 10, Vladimir Melnik, bottom 18, Volina, 8, Volonoff, design element, WanderDream, bottom 21, wildestanimal, top 11, top left 18, Willyam Bradberry, top right 23

Every effort has been made to contact copyright holders of material reproduced in this book. Any omissions will be rectified in subsequent printings if notice is given to the publisher.

Contents

Words in **bold** are in the glossary.

Chapter 1

Earth's oceans

About 70 per cent of Earth is covered by oceans. Let's dive in and explore this amazing underwater world!

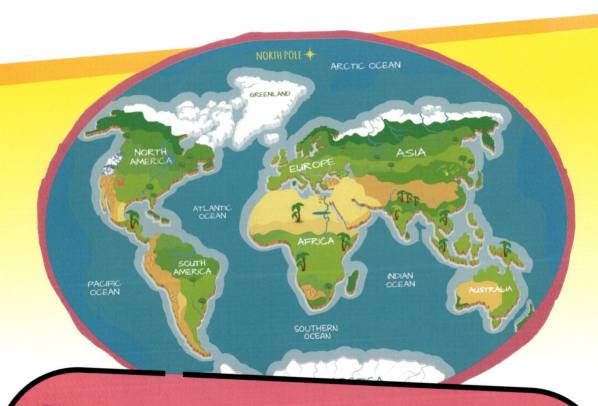

There is one big ocean on Earth. It is divided into five smaller oceans: Atlantic, Arctic, Indian, Pacific and Southern. But they are all connected.

The ocean holds 97 per cent of all the water on Earth.

The ocean gives us about 70 per cent of the gas we need to breathe – **oxygen**.

Earth is the only planet known to have liquid water.

Only 5 per cent of the world's oceans have been explored.

Scientists believe most ocean animals haven't been discovered yet!

shaggy frogfish

Oceans stop our planet from getting too hot or too cold.

The ocean is warmed by the sun. The water **evaporates** and floats up to the sky. There it can turn into rain and storms.

Chapter 2

Pacific Ocean

The Pacific is the largest ocean. It is bigger than all of Earth's **continents** combined!

The Pacific Ocean lies between North America, Asia and Australia.

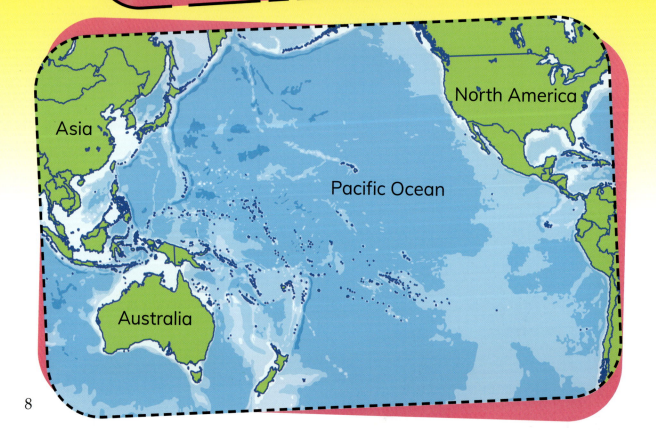

The Pacific Ocean covers more than 30 per cent of Earth.

There are more than 25,000 islands in the Pacific Ocean.

Mount Everest

Mariana Trench

Mariana Trench, the deepest place on Earth, is in the Pacific Ocean. It is almost 11.3 kilometres (7 miles) deep. Mount Everest could fit inside!

Most of Earth's volcanoes are found underwater in the Pacific Ocean. They form a circle known as the "Ring of Fire".

Ring of Fire

underwater volcano

Kelp, coral, sea grass and phytoplankton are a few types of plants found in the Pacific Ocean.

coral

orca

Dolphins, orcas and fish, including sharks, live in the Pacific Ocean.

The giant Pacific octopus is the largest octopus in the world.

Chapter 3

Atlantic Ocean

The Atlantic is the second-largest ocean. It is home to the longest mountain range on Earth!

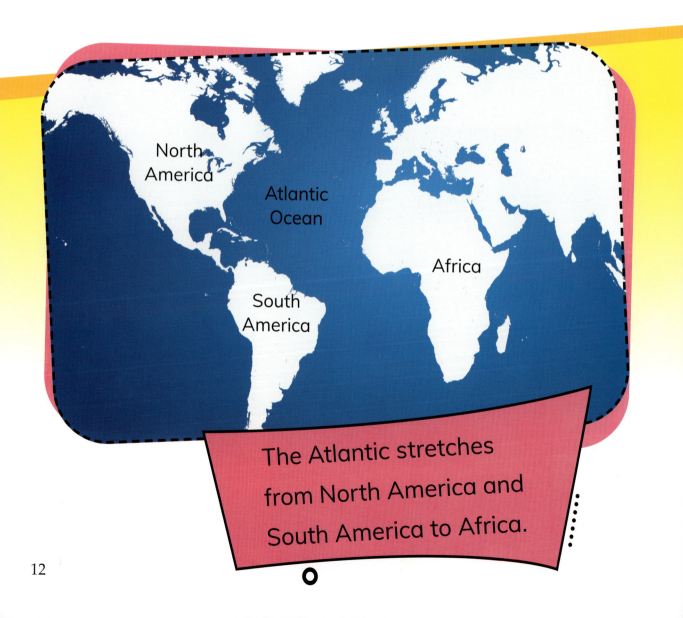

North America

Atlantic Ocean

Africa

South America

The Atlantic stretches from North America and South America to Africa.

Earth's **equator** divides the Atlantic Ocean into two parts – the North Atlantic and South Atlantic.

On average, the Atlantic Ocean is about 3,658 metres (12,000 feet) deep. That's about the length of 33 football pitches!

The Mid-Atlantic Ridge mountain range is on the floor of the Atlantic. The top can be seen in Iceland.

Mid-Atlantic crest in Iceland

The Atlantic was the first ocean to be crossed by ship and aeroplane.

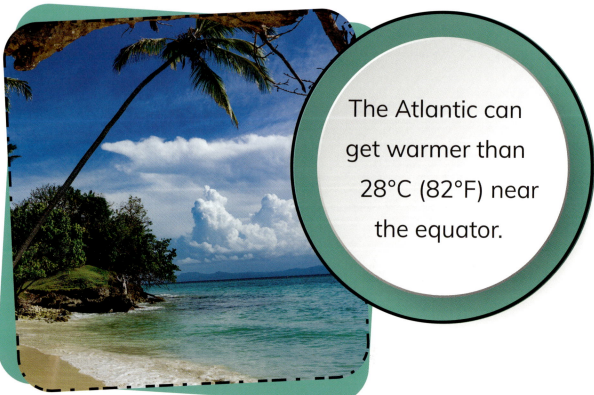

The Atlantic can get warmer than 28°C (82°F) near the equator.

Walruses, manatees, great white sharks and humpback whales all live in the Atlantic.

manatee

great white shark

The Mesoamerican Reef in the Atlantic is the second-biggest barrier **reef** in the world.

Chapter 4

Arctic Ocean

The Arctic is the smallest ocean. It is also the coldest and shallowest. Much of it is covered by ice.

The United States, Canada, Russia, Norway, Greenland and Iceland border the Arctic Ocean.

The Arctic Ocean has an average depth of 1,038 m (3,406 feet). You could stack three Eiffel Towers at the bottom and still not reach the surface!

The Arctic Ocean is about −2°C (28°F) all year round.

The Arctic Ocean covers less than 3 per cent of Earth's surface.

polar bears

Walruses, beluga whales, narwhals, polar bears and seals are found in the Arctic Ocean.

walruses

narwhals

The Arctic is nicknamed the "Frozen Ocean".

Because of Earth's tilt, the Arctic Ocean is in total darkness for one day each year.

beluga whale

The North Pole is the northernmost point on Earth. It's in the middle of the Arctic Ocean.

Chapter 5

Indian Ocean

The Indian Ocean is the third-largest ocean. But it's still huge! It covers almost 20 per cent of Earth's surface.

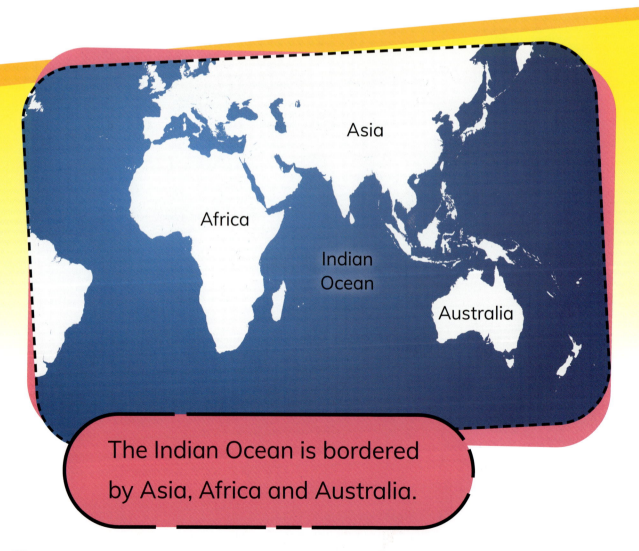

Asia

Africa

Indian Ocean

Australia

The Indian Ocean is bordered by Asia, Africa and Australia.

The Indian Ocean is the warmest ocean in the world.

The Indian Ocean is so warm that fewer plants and animals can live there.

The largest **bay** in the world, the Bay of Bengal, is in the Indian Ocean.

The Indian Ocean is more than twice as deep as the Grand Canyon.

More than 7,000 humpback whales travel to the Indian Ocean every year to give birth.

blue whale

dolphins

Blue whales, dolphins, clown fish and starfish live in the Indian Ocean.

clown fish

starfish

Chapter 6

Southern Ocean

The Southern Ocean is the fourth-largest ocean. It's a very cloudy and windy place!

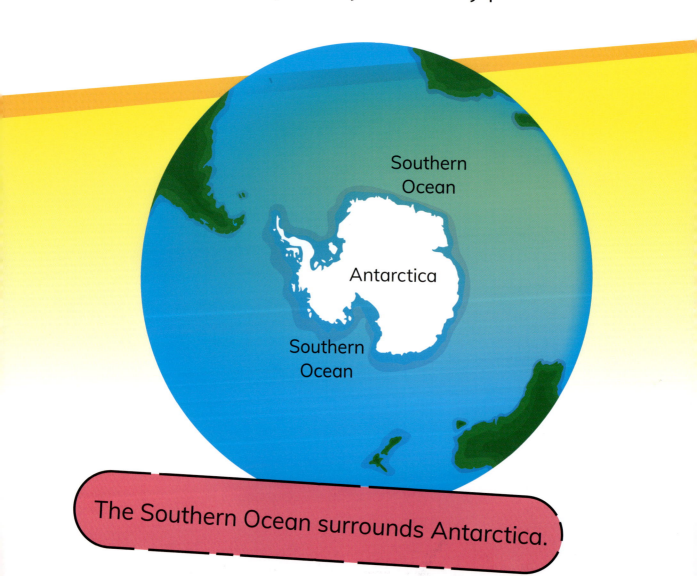

Southern Ocean

Antarctica

Southern Ocean

The Southern Ocean surrounds Antarctica.

The Southern Ocean is the youngest ocean. It formed 30 million years ago.

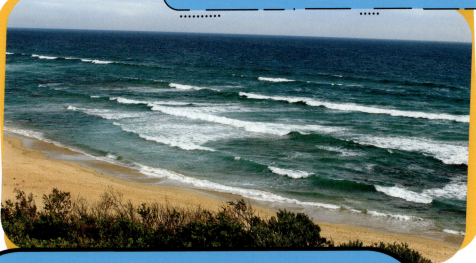

The temperature of the Southern Ocean ranges from −2°C (28°F) to 10°C (50°F).

The deepest part is called the South Sandwich Trench. It is more than 6.4 km (4 miles) deep.

In winter, almost half of the Southern Ocean is covered with ice.

Some of the strongest winds in the world blow over the Southern Ocean.

Emperor penguins

Emperor penguins, fur seals and giant squid live in the Southern Ocean.

fur seal

There are not many types of fish found in the Southern Ocean.

Chapter 7

Protecting our oceans

We depend on the oceans for the air we breathe, water we drink and food we eat. It's important to take care of them!

Too many fish are being taken out of the ocean. Animals such as whales and dolphins won't have enough food.

Tonnes of plastic and other rubbish is floating in an area called the Great Pacific Garbage Patch.

oil spill

Large ships carrying oil can be dangerous. The oil can spill into the ocean and hurt the animals that live there.

The ice in the Arctic Ocean is melting. Many animals can't survive without the ice.

Use a reusable water bottle instead of a plastic one.

Join organised litter picks to help keep the beach clean.

Recycle everything you can.

Learn all you can about the ocean. The more you know, the more you'll be able to help!

Glossary

bay part of the ocean that is partly closed in by land

continent one of Earth's seven large land masses

equator imaginary line around the middle of Earth

evaporate change from a liquid to a gas

oxygen colourless gas in the air; humans and animals need oxygen to live

reef underwater strip of rocks, coral or sand near the surface of the ocean

Index